What's in this book

This book belongs to

T0351511

_____

捉迷藏 Hide-and-seek

学习内容 Contents

沟通 Communication

询问方位
Ask about position

说出方位
Say the position

数一至一百
Count from one to one hundred

背景介绍：
浩浩和玲玲在玩捉迷藏游戏。

生词 New words

★	上面	up
★	下面	down
★	前面	front
★	后面	back
★	哪里	where
★	在	at, in
★	百	hundred
★	门	door
	窗	window
	沙发	sofa
	桌子	table

句式 Sentence patterns

爸爸在哪里？	Where is Dad?
他在沙发后面。	He is behind the sofa.
玲玲在哪里？	Where is Ling Ling?
她在桌子下面。	She is under the table.

跨学科学习 Project

制作纸房子，描述门窗方位
Make a paper house and say the
positions of the door and the window

文化 Cultures

北京城中以城门命名的地方
Places named after the city gates
in Beijing

参考答案：
1 Yes, I do./No, I don't. I can never find a good place to hide.
2 I usually play with my friends/cousins.
3 I like to hide under the bed/in the garden.

Get ready

1 Do you like playing hide-and-seek?

2 Who do you usually play this game with?

3 Where do you like to hide?

jiǔ shí jiǔ yī bǎi
九十九、一百！

"百"是数名，十个十。

故事大意：
浩浩、玲玲、爸爸和布朗尼在玩捉迷藏。浩浩找到了爸爸和玲玲，但怎么也找不着布朗尼，最后成功用食物将它引了出来。

参考问题和答案：
1 What is Hao Hao doing? (He is counting.)
2 What are Ling Ling and Dad doing? (They are finding somewhere to hide.)

我爱捉迷藏。"一、二、三……九十九、一百！"

在哪里?
zài nǎ li

"在"用来表示人或事物的位置,如:在家、在学校。而当我们想知道某个人或事物的位置时,可以用"哪里"来提问。

沙发
shā fā

"沙发"是个外来词,是由英语单词sofa音译过来的。

后面
hòu mian

爸爸在哪里? 他在沙发后面。

参考问题和答案:
1 Who did Hao Hao find? (He found Dad.)
2 Where is Dad hiding? (He is hiding behind the sofa.)

zhuō zi
桌子

xià mian
下面

姐姐在哪里？她在桌子
下面。

参考问题和答案：
1 Who did Hao Hao find? (He found Ling Ling.)
2 Where is Ling Ling hiding? (She is hiding under the table.)

búù

参考问题和答案：

1 Who are Hao Hao and Ling Ling looking for? (They are looking for Brownie.)
2 Where are they looking? (They are looking for it behind the door and under the window.)

小狗在哪里？它不在门后面，也不在窗下面。

参考问题和答案：
1　Why is Hao Hao taking out some biscuits? (Be⋯ he wants to use them to lure Brownie out.)
2　Where is Hao Hao putting the biscuits? (He is putting them on the table.)

shàng mian
上面

"上面"和"下面"是反义词。

我有办法。"布朗尼，
饼干在桌子上面。"

前面

"前面"和"后面"是反义词。

布朗尼在我们前面。

参考问题和答案：

1　Did Hao Hao's trick work? (Yes, it did.)

2　Where is Brownie? (It is in front of Hao Hao, Ling Ling and Dad.)

Let's think

1 Recall the story. Put a tick or a cross.

2 Play hide-and-seek with your friends. Tick the place where you would hide and say. 学生勾选出自己想躲藏的地方，再描述该位置，如"我在桌子下面。""我在门后面。""我在沙发后面。"

New words

1 Learn the new words.

门　窗　桌子　后面　前面　沙发　百　哪里　在　上面　下面

2 Match the sentences to the pictures. Write the letters.

a 她在上面。b 他在下面。

a 她在后面。b 他在前面。

听听说说 Listen and say

第一题录音稿：
1 小狗在桌子下面喝水。
2 姐姐在沙发上面吃苹果
3 一百

03 **1** Listen and circle the correct pictures.

04 **2** Look at the pictures. Listen to

1

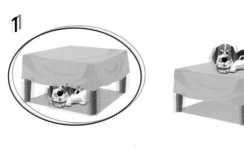

2

3

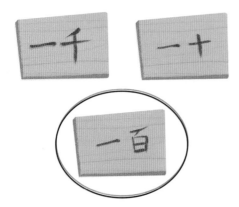

第二题参考问题和答案：
1　What are the children doing? (They are having a sports day.)
2　Have you ever taken part in any events in your school sports day? (Yes, I have.
　　I was the winner of the 100-metre race./No, I have not. I am not good at sports.)

...y and say.

3　Help Hao Hao find his book. Write the letters and say.

a 上面　　b 后面
c 前面　　d 下面

书在哪里？

书在桌子＿＿a＿＿。
书在窗＿＿d＿＿。

Task

Paste a photo of your room and talk about it.

桌子在前面，窗在后面。
足球在沙发上面。

Paste your photo here.

Game

Something is wrong in the crime scene. Write the numbers and report.

可提高题目难度，让学生写中文数字。

窗下面有 ___二___ 只鸟。

桌子上面有 ___六___ 本书。

沙发前面有 ___二___ 个足球。

沙发后面有 ___三___ 条鱼。

Song

延伸活动：
学唱歌前可以让学生玩一个热身游戏，加深对"上面""下面""前面"和"后面"四个方位词的印象。学生两人一组，一个人说任意一个方位词，另一个快速用手势表示该方位（如"上面"用手指指着天花板）。下一轮则两人互换角色。

05 **Listen and sing.**

上面下面前面后面，

我们玩捉迷藏。

我在沙发后面，

他在桌子下面。

你数一二三，

我数四五六，

七八九十，

开始啦！开始啦！

课堂用语 Classroom language

交给我。

Please give it to me.

一起做。

Let's do it together.

15

Write

1 **Learn and trace the stroke.** 老师示范笔画动作，学生跟着做：用手在空中画出"点"。

点

2 **Learn the component. Trace 门 in the characters.**

门　闷　们　问

引导学生发现"门"字与大门有关。

3 **How are the characters related to 门? Match and discuss with your friend.**

告诉学生四个字的意思，再让学生两人一组讨论。问：发问；闷：心情不舒畅；间：本义是"空隙、缝隙"；闪：本义是"在门缝中偷看"。

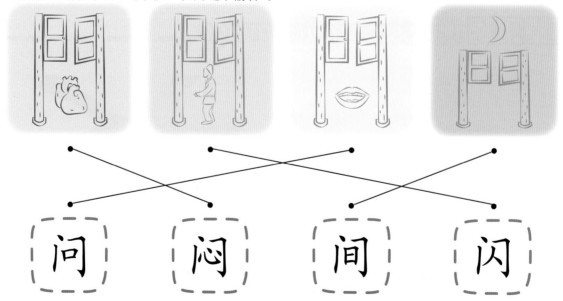

问　闷　间　闪

"问"是门口有一张嘴，所以是有人站在门外对里边的人张嘴问问题；"闷"是心被关在门内，所以心情不舒畅；"间"是门的上方有一轮弯月，表示从门缝中看月亮，所以意思是"空隙、缝隙"；"闪"是一个人在门缝中偷看，引申指忽隐忽现或者突然显现。

4 Trace and write the character.

ノ イ イ イ 们

们 们 们

5 Write and say.

问问学生，图中有多少个人，以及当称呼包括自己在内的几个人时需要用哪个词。

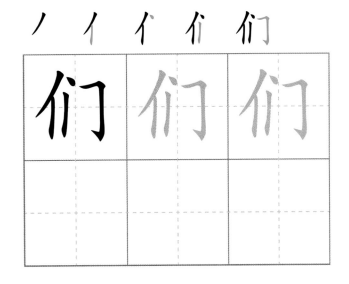

我 们 玩捉迷藏。

汉字小常识 Did you know?

Guess what these characters mean.
Write the letters.

Some characters look like symbols which give clues to their meanings.

a 下　b 二　c 上　d 一　e 三

| c | d | a | b | e |

学生先根据图形和文字的形状将两者配对，再根据图形猜测文字意思。"一"是一横画，表示数字"1"，"二"和"三"同理，分别表示数字"2"和"3"；"上"字的图形是一条弧线上面有一横，表示位置在高处；"下"字的图形相反，一横在弧线下面，意思也与"上"相反。

Cultures

北京城门分为宫城城门、皇城城门、内城城门、外城城门四类。图中，午门为宫城城门，位于紫禁城正门；天安门为皇城城门，位于皇城正门；内城有九个城门，分别为前门、崇文门、朝阳门、东直门、安定门、德胜门、西直门、阜城门、宣武门；外城有七个城门，分别为永定门、左安门、广渠门、东便门、西便门、广安门、右安门。

There are many places in Beijing named after 门. How many 门 can you find?

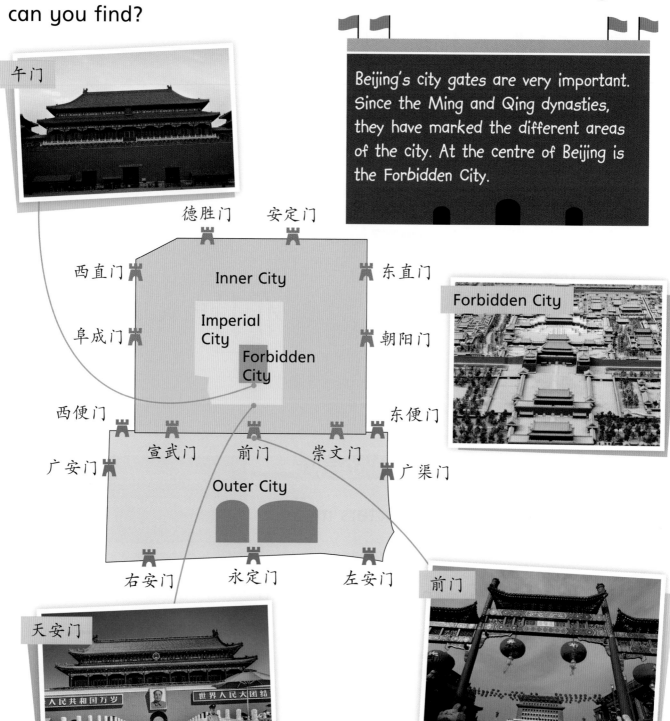

午门

Beijing's city gates are very important. Since the Ming and Qing dynasties, they have marked the different areas of the city. At the centre of Beijing is the Forbidden City.

德胜门　安定门

西直门　　Inner City　　东直门

Forbidden City

Imperial City

阜成门　Forbidden City　朝阳门

西便门　　　　　　　东便门

广安门　宣武门　前门　崇文门　广渠门

Outer City

右安门　永定门　左安门

前门

天安门

人民共和国万岁　世界人民大团结

Project

材料：
彩笔、五张硬卡纸、一把剪刀、一瓶胶水。

1 Make a paper house.

用另外两张硬卡纸画左右两面墙。根据前后墙的宽度在左右墙的两边留下适当边缘，以便粘贴。

在两张硬卡纸上画出屋子的前后两面，并裁剪下来。

用胶水将四面墙粘贴在一起。

将最后一张硬卡纸对折，作为屋顶，粘在墙的上方。

纸屋做好了！

2 Show your paper house to your friend and talk about it.

门在前面，窗在上面和下面，沙发在里面。

1 Follow the instructions on the doors to get the treasure chest.

游戏方法：

学生按照大门上的号码线索，依次完成对应的题目，走到迷宫出口，回答了最后一道问题便可取得宝箱。

① 👄 前面

② Say 'door' in Chinese. 门

③ Complete the word 'we' in Chinese.

我 们

④ Say 'on the sofa' in Chinese.

在沙发上面

⑤ 👄 爸爸在哪里？

⑥  这是什么？　这是"门"。

⑦ Say '100' in Chinese. 百

⑧ Where is the treasure chest? Answer in Chinese.

它在桌子下面。

评核方法：
学生两人一组，互相考察评价表内单词和句子的听说读写。交际沟通部分由老师朗读要求，学生再互相对话。
如果达到了某项技能要求，则用色笔将星星或小辣椒涂色。

2 Work with your friend. Colour the stars and the chillies.

Words	说	读	写
上面	☆	☆	🌶
下面	☆	★	🌶
前面	☆	☆	🌶
后面	☆	☆	🌶
哪里	☆	☆	🌶
在	☆	☆	🌶
百	☆	☆	🌶
门	☆	☆	☆
窗	☆	🌶	🌶

Words and sentences	说	读	写
沙发	☆	🌶	🌶
桌子	☆	🌶	🌶
爸爸在哪里？	☆	★	🌶
他在沙发后面。	☆	🌶	🌶

Ask about position	☆
Say the position	☆
Count from one to one hundred	☆

3 What does your teacher say?

My teacher says ...

评核建议：
根据学生课堂表现，分别给予"太棒了！(Excellent!)"、
"不错！(Good!)"或"继续努力！(Work harder!)"的评价，
再让学生圈出上方对应的表情，以记录自己的学习情况。

分享 Sharing

延伸活动：
1 学生用手遮盖英文，读中文单词，并思考单词意思；
2 学生用手遮盖中文单词，看着英文说出对应的中文单词；
3 学生三人一组，尽量运用中文单词复述故事。

Words I remember

上面	shàng mian	up
下面	xià mian	down
前面	qián mian	front
后面	hòu mian	back
哪里	nǎ li	where
在	zài	at, in
百	bǎi	hundred
门	mén	door
窗	chuāng	window
沙发	shā fā	sofa
桌子	zhuō zi	table

Other words

爱	ài	to love
捉迷藏	zhuō mí cáng	hide-and-seek
也	yě	also
有	yǒu	to have
办法	bàn fǎ	solution
饼干	bǐng gān	biscuit

OXFORD

UNIVERSITY PRESS

Oxford University Press is a department of the University of Oxford.
It furthers the University's objective of excellence in research, scholarship,
and education by publishing worldwide. Oxford is a registered trade mark of
Oxford University Press in the UK and in certain other countries

Published in Hong Kong by
Oxford University Press (China) Limited
39th Floor, One Kowloon, 1 Wang Yuen Street, Kowloon Bay,
Hong Kong

© Oxford University Press (China) Limited 2017

The moral rights of the author have been asserted

First Edition published in 2017

Illustrated by Anne Lee and Wildman

Photographs for reproduction permitted by Dreamstime.com

China National Publications Import & Export (Group) Corporation is an authorized distributor of
Oxford Elementary Chinese.

Please contact content@cnpiec.com.cn or 86-10-65856782

ISBN: 978-0-19-942982-0

10 9 8 7 6 5 4 3 2

Teacher's Edition
ISBN: 978-0-19-082204-0

10 9 8 7 6 5 4 3 2